The Key to Success

100 POWERFUL DUʿĀ
FROM THE QURAN
& SUNNAH

The Key to Success

100 POWERFUL DU'Ā FROM THE QURAN & SUNNAH

Mohsen Elbeltagi

1 2 3 4 5 6 7 8 9 10

All rights reserved. No part of this publication may be reproduced, stored in a retrieval system or transmitted in any form or by any means – electronic, mechanical, photocopying, recording or otherwise – without written permission from the publisher.

© Light Publishing 2022

Mohsen Elbeltagi

The Key to Success:
100 Powerful Duʿā from the Quran & Sunnah

ISBN 978-1-915570-22-2

www.lightpublishing.co.uk

بسم الله الرحمن الرحيم

CONTENTS

INTRODUCTION 9

Seeking Forgiveness 13
Glorification & Remembrance of Allah ﷻ 21
Seeking Protection & Relief 27
Seeking Guidance, Benefit & Blessings 41

INTRODUCTION

Challenges, aspirations and worries are an inescapable part of everyday life. We plan, we prepare, we train and we strategize, reading countless self-help books that seek to convince us of the best ways to achieve whatever it is that we're looking for.

Whilst acknowledging the wisdom and benefit of such sources, we must realise that the most powerful and effective self-help tool we've been gifted is the ability to make du'ā (supplication). True success lies with Allah ﷻ alone, and He has provided us with the perfect tool to gain ultimate success in this life and the next.

Unlike regular self-help tools, making du'ā relies on the acknowledgement of our complete inability to succeed without aid. It's the manifestation of one's true reliance and trust in Allah ﷻ as the Disposer of Affairs and the One in Whose Hands our whole lives rest. Nothing can happen without the aid and permission of Allah ﷻ. And it is only through glorifying Him, seeking His help and begging for His forgiveness that we will achieve true success.

This book contains a selection of powerful supplications that can be made to achieve success in this life and the hereafter. All supplications have been sourced from the Quran and sunnah of Prophet Muhammad ﷺ as recorded in the authentic Hadith collections. Each du'ā is included with its translation[1], along with its English transliteration to help those who don't

---

[1] All translations of the Quran have been taken from Sahih International

have knowledge of the Arabic language.

Based on the meanings of the du'ā, the book has been divided into four general sections: Seeking Forgiveness, Glorifying & Remembering Allah, Seeking Protection & Relief and Seeking Guidance, Benefit & Blessings.

Seeking Forgiveness
The book begins with a plea for forgiveness because although du'ā is the most powerful tool we have to achieving success in this life and the hereafter, the magnitude of its power depends upon the righteousness of its caller; sins can inhibit the effectiveness of your du'ā, standing between you and its acceptance.

Ibn al-Qayyim said,

> Du'ā and the seeking of protection from Allah are like weapons, but the sharpness of a weapon is not sufficient for it to cause effect for the person that handles it also plays a role. So whenever the weapon is a perfect one, having no flaw in it, and the forearm is strong, and there are no preventing factors, then it will cause an effect on the enemy...[2]

Glorification & Remembrance of Allah
The book continues with a collection of du'ā that focus on glorifying and remembering Allah through his names, attributes and favours. The benefits and wisdoms behind such remembrances are endless and far too many to mention here, but it will suffice to say that such du'ā bring reward, forgiveness, increased faith, and Allah's pleasure and closeness. Allah says,

> "So remember Me, I will remember you"
>
> [Quran 2:152]

---

2   Cited in: Qadir, Yasir. *"Dua: The Weapon of the Believer"*. A-Hidāyah Publishing and Distribution Ltd. 2003. p.3.

"Unquestionably, by the remembrance of Allah, hearts are assured."

[Quran 13:28]

The Messenger of Allah ﷺ said,

"Shall I not inform you of the best of your actions, the purest in the sight of your Lord, which raises your rank to the highest, which is better for you than spending gold and silver, better than meeting your enemy so that you strike at their necks and they strike at yours? They replied, 'Yes, indeed', and he said, 'It is the remembrance of Allah' ".

(al-Tirmidhi)

Seeking Protection & Relief

Du'ā is a cure, relief and prevention for all ailments and hardships, both physical and spiritual. Ibn al-Qayyim said,

Du'ā is of the most beneficial cures, and it is the enemy of all diseases. It fights them, and cures them, and prevents their occurrence, and causes them to be raised up or reduced after its occurrence. It is the weapon of the believer.[3]

As such, the book continues with a collection of du'ā that seek refuge in Allah ﷻ from trials, tribulations, ailments and concerns both in this life and the hereafter.

Seeking Guidance, Benefit & Blessings

Identifying Allah ﷻ as the source of all good and the Most Generous (al-Karīm), the book ends with a collection of du'ā, both general and specific, that ask Allah ﷻ for guidance, benefit and blessings in this world and the hereafter.

---

3 Cited in: Qadir, Yasir. "*Dua: The Weapon of the Believer*". A-Hidāyah Publishing and Distribution Ltd. 2003. p.56.

SEEKING FORGIVENESS

(1)

أَسْتَغْفِرُ اللهَ

Astaghfirullāh

I seek the forgiveness of Allah.

Source: Abu Dawud, Ibn Maja and others.

---

(2)

اللَّهُمَّ إِنِّي أَسْأَلُكَ يَا اللَّهُ الأَحَدُ الصَّمَدُ الَّذِي لَمْ يَلِدْ وَلَمْ يُولَدْ وَلَمْ يَكُنْ لَهُ كُفُوًا أَحَدٌ أَنْ تَغْفِرَ لِي ذُنُوبِي إِنَّكَ أَنْتَ الْغَفُورُ الرَّحِيمُ

Allāhumma innī asa'luka yā allāhul-ahadus-samad, alladhī lam yalid wa lamyūlad wa-lam yakul-lahu kufuwan ahad, an taghfira lī dhunūbī innaka antal-ghafūrur-rahīm

O Allah, I ask You [because I testify that] You are Allah, the Only One, Self-Sufficient. The one who begets not and nor is He begotten, and there is no one like Him. Forgive me my sins. Indeed, You are the Most Forgiving, The Merciful.

Source: Abu Dawud

---

(3)

اللَّهمَّ اغفِر لي ذنبي وأخسئ شيطاني ، وفُكَّ رِهاني وثَقِّل ميزاني واجعَلني في النَّديِّ الأعلى

Allāhumma-ghfir lī dhanbi wa akhsi' shaytāni wa fukka rihāni waj'alnī finnadiyyil-a'lā

O Allah, forgive my sins and keep my devil away from me and free me from my burdens and place me in the highest assembly.

Source: Sunan Abu-Dawud

---

(4)

اللَّهُمَّ أَنْتَ رَبِّي لا إلهَ إلاَّ أَنْتَ خَلَقْتَنِي وَأَنَا عَبْدُكَ ، وَأَنَا عَلَى عَهْدِكَ وَوَعْدِكَ مَا اسْتَطَعْتُ أَعُوذُبِكَ مِنْ شَرِّ مَا صَنَعْتُ أَبُوءُ لَكَ بِنِعْمَتِكَ عَلَيَّ وَأَبُوءُ بِذَنْبِي فَاغْفِرْ لِي فَإِنَّهُ لا يَغْفِرُ الذُّنوبَ إِلاَّ أَنْتَ

Allāhumma anta rabbī lā ilāha illā ant, khalaqtanī wa anā 'abduka wa anā 'alā 'ahdika wa w'adika mastat'at, a'ūdhu bika min sharri mā san'at, abūu' laka bin'imatika 'alayy, wa abūu' laka bi-dhambi faghfir lī fa innahu lā yaghfirud-dhunnuba illā ant

O Allah, You are my Lord, there is no God (worthy of worship) but You. You created me and I am Your slave. And I am committed in my pledge to You and in my promise to You to the best of my ability. I seek refuge in You from the evil of my deeds. I acknowledge (recognize) Your blessings on me and I acknowledge (recognize) my sins. So forgive me as no one forgives sins but You.

Source: Sahih al-Bukhari

---

(5)

اللَّهُمَّ اغْفِرْ لِي ذَنْبِي كُلَّهُ دِقَّهُ وَجِلَّهُ وَأَوَّلَهُ وَآخِرَهُ وَعَلَانِيَتَهُ وَسِرَّهُ

Allāhummaghfir lī dhambi kullahu diqqahu wajillahu wa awwalahu wa ākhirahu wa'alāniyatahu wa sirrah

O Allah, forgive all of my sins, the small and the big, the first and the last and the ones that are known and the ones that are in secret.

Source: Sahih Muslim

---

(6)

اللّهُمَّ إِنِّي ظَلَمْتُ نَفْسِي ظُلْمًا كَثِيرًا، وَلَا يَغْفِرُ الذُّنُوبَ إِلَّا أَنْتَ، فَاغْفِرْ لِي مَغْفِرَةً مِنْ عِنْدِكَ، وَارْحَمْنِي، إِنَّكَ أَنْتَ الْغَفُورُ الرَّحِيمُ

Allāhumma innī zalamtu nafsī zulman kathīrā, walā yaghfirudh-dhunūba illā ant, faghfir lī maghfiratan min 'indika warhamnī, innaka antal-ghafūrur-rahīm

O Allah, I have oppressed myself with many wrongs, and none can forgive sins but You. So grant me forgiveness from Your forgiveness and have mercy on me. You are the Most Merciful and The Forgiving.

Source: Sahih al-Bukhari

---

(7)

رَبَّنَا ظَلَمْنَا أَنْفُسَنَا وَإِنْ لَمْ تَغْفِرْ لَنَا وَتَرْحَمْنَا لَنَكُونَنَّ مِنَ الْخَاسِرِينَ

Rabbanā zalamnā anfusanā wa il-lam taghfir lanā wa tarhamnā lanakūnanna minal-khāsirīn

Our Lord, we have wronged ourselves, and if You do not forgive us and have mercy upon us, we will surely be among the losers.

Source: Quran (7:23)

---

(8)

اللَّهُمَّ إِنَّكَ عَفُوٌّ تُحِبُّ الْعَفْوَ فَاعْفُ عَنِّي

Allāhumma innaka 'afuwwun tuhibbul-'afwa fa'fu 'annī

O Allah, You are the One who pardons. You love to pardon, so pardon me.

Source: al-Tirmidhi

---

(9)

اللَّهُمَّ بَاعِدْ بَيْنِي وَبَيْنَ خَطَايَايَ كَمَا بَاعَدْتَ بَيْنَ الْمَشْرِقِ وَالْمَغْرِبِ اللَّهُمَّ نَقِّنِي مِنَ الْخَطَايَا كَمَا يُنَقَّى الثَّوْبُ الْأَبْيَضُ مِنَ الدَّنَسِ اللَّهُمَّ اغْسِلْنِي مِنْ خَطَايَايَ بِالْمَاءِ وَالثَّلْجِ وَالْبَرَدِ

Allāhumma bā'id baynī wa-bayna khatāyāya kamā bā'adta baynal-mashriqi wal-maghrib, Allāhumma naqqinī min khatāyā

*kamā yunaqqa-aththawbul-abyadu minad-danas, Allāhumma-
ghsilnī min khatāya bil-māi' wath-thalji wal-barad*

O Allah, distance (separate) me from my sins as the East and
the West are set apart from eachother. O Allah, cleanse me
from my sins as a white garment is cleansed from dirt. O
Allah, wash off my sins with water, snow and hail.

Source: al-Bukhari

---

(10)

اللَّهُمَّ أَنْتَ المَلِكُ لا إِلَهَ إِلَّا أَنْتَ، أَنْتَ رَبِّي وَأَنَا عَبْدُكَ، ظَلَمْتُ نَفْسِي، وَاعْتَرَفْتُ بِذَنْبِي، فَاغْفِرْ لِي ذُنُوبِي جَمِيعًا، إِنَّهُ لا يَغْفِرُ الذُّنُوبَ إِلَّا أَنْتَ، وَاهْدِنِي لأَحْسَنِ الأَخْلاقِ، لا يَهْدِي لأَحْسَنِهَا إِلَّا أَنْتَ، وَاصْرِفْ عَنِّي سَيِّئَهَا، لا يَصْرِفُ عَنِّي سَيِّئَهَا إِلَّا أَنْتَ، وَسَعْدَيْكَ، لَبَّيْكَ، وَالْخَيْرُ كُلُّهُ فِي يَدَيْكَ، وَالشَّرُّ لَيْسَ إِلَيْكَ، أَنَا بِكَ وَإِلَيْكَ، تَبَارَكْتَ وَتَعَالَيْتَ، أَسْتَغْفِرُكَ وَأَتُوبُ إِلَيْكَ.

*Allāhumma antal-maliku lā ilāha illā ant, anta rabbī wa anā
'abduka zalamtu nafsī, w'ataraftu bidhanbī, faghfir lī dhunūbī
jamī'ā, innahu lā yaghfirudh- dhunūba illā ant, Allāhummahdinī li-ahsanil-akhlāq, lā yahdī liahsanihā illā ant, wasrif 'annī
sayyia'hā, lā yasrifu 'annī sayyia'hā illā ant, labbayka wa s'adayka
wal-khayru kulluhu fī yadayk, wash-sharru laysa ilayk, anā bika
wa ilayk, tabārakta wa ta'ālayt, astaghfiruka wa atūbu ilayk*

O Allah, You are the King and there is no God (worthy of
worship) but You. You are my Lord and I am Your slave. I
have wronged myself and I acknowledge and admit my sins.
So forgive all my sins, as no one can forgive (my sins) but
You. O Allah, guide me toward the best of character and
manners, as no one guides to its best but You. And keep sins
away from me, as no one can keep sins away from me but
You. Here I am at your service and pleasing you, and all good
is in Your Hands and evil is not attributed to You. We are
from You and will return to You. You are blessed and exalted.
I seek Your forgiveness and turn to You in repentance.

Source: Muslim

(11)

اللّٰهُـمَّ اغْفِـرْ لِي مَا قَدَّمْتُ وَمَا أَخَّـرْتُ، وَمَا أَسْرَرْتُ وَمَا أَعْلَنْتُ، وَمَا أَنْتَ أَعْلَمُ بِهِ مِنِّـي، أَنْـتَ المُقَدِّمُ وَأَنْتَ المُؤَخِّرُ، لَا إِلَهَ إِلَّا أنتَ

Allāhummaghfir lī mā qaddamtu wa mā akh-khartu wa mā asrartu wa mā 'alantu wa mā asraftu wa mā anta 'alamu bihī minnī, antal-muqaddimu wa antal-muakh-khiru lā ilāha illā ant

O Allah, forgive me for the earlier and the later (sins) and that what I did in secret and in the open and that which I did in excess and that about which You know better than I. You are The Expeditor and You are The Delayer. There is no God (worthy of worship) but You.

Source: Muslim

---

(12)

رَبَّنَـا إِنَّنَا آمَنَّا فَاغْفِـرْ لَنَا ذُنُوبَنَا وَقِنَا عَذَابَ النَّارِ

Rabbanā innanā āmannā faghfir lanā dhunūbanā wa qinā 'athāban-nār

Our Lord, indeed we have believed, so forgive us our sins and protect us from the punishment of the Fire.

Source: Quran (3:16)

---

(13)

رَبَّنَا إِنَّنَا سَمِعْنَا مُنَادِيًا يُنَادِي لِلْإِيمَانِ أَنْ آمِنُوا بِرَبِّكُمْ فَآمَنَّا رَبَّنَا فَاغْفِرْ لَنَا ذُنُوبَنَا وَكَفِّرْ عَنَّا سَيِّئَاتِنَا وَتَوَفَّنَا مَعَ الْأَبْرَارِ

Rabbanā innanā sam'ina munādiyan yunadī lilīmāni an āminū birabbikum fa-āmannā rabbanā faghfir lanā dhunūbanā wakaffir 'annā say-yiātinā wa tawaffanā ma'al-abrār

Our Lord, indeed we have heard a caller calling to faith, [saying], 'Believe in your Lord,' and we have believed. Our Lord, so forgive us our sins and remove from us our misdeeds and cause us to die with the righteous.

Source: Quran (3:193)

(14)

رَبَّنَا اغْفِرْ لِي وَلِوَالِدَيَّ وَلِلْمُؤْمِنِينَ يَوْمَ يَقُومُ الْحِسَابُ

Rabbanaghfir lī wa liwālidayya wa lilmu'minīna yawma yaqūmul-hisāb

Our Lord, forgive me and my parents and the believers the Day the account is established.

Source: Quran (14:41)

---

(15)

رَّبِّ اغْفِرْ وَارْحَمْ وَأَنتَ خَيْرُ الرَّاحِمِينَ

Rabbighfir warham wa anta khayrur-rāhimīn

My Lord, forgive and have mercy, and You are the best of the merciful.

Source: Quran (23:118)

---

(16)

رَبِّ إِنِّي ظَلَمْتُ نَفْسِي فَاغْفِرْ لِي

Rabbi innī zalamtu nafsī faghfir lī

My Lord, indeed I have wronged myself, so forgive me.

Source: Quran (28:16)

---

(17)

رَبَّنَا اغْفِرْ لَنَا وَلِإِخْوَانِنَا الَّذِينَ سَبَقُونَا بِالْإِيمَانِ وَلَا تَجْعَلْ فِي قُلُوبِنَا غِلًّا لِّلَّذِينَ آمَنُوا رَبَّنَا إِنَّكَ رَءُوفٌ رَّحِيمٌ

Rabbanaghfir lanā wa li-ikhwāninā al-ladhīna sadbaqūnā bil-īmani wa lā taj'al fī qulūbinā ghil-lan lil-ladhīna āmanū rabbanā innaka raūfur-rahīm

Our Lord, forgive us and our brothers who preceded us in faith and put not in our hearts [any] resentment toward those who have believed. Our Lord, indeed You are Kind and Merciful.

Source: Quran (59:10)

---

(18)

رَّبِّ اغْفِرْ لِي وَلِوَالِدَيَّ وَلِمَن دَخَلَ بَيْتِيَ مُؤْمِنًا وَلِلْمُؤْمِنِينَ وَالْمُؤْمِنَاتِ وَلَا تَزِدِ الظَّالِمِينَ إِلَّا تَبَارًا

Rabbighfirlī waliwālidayya waliman dakhala baytiya mu'minan wa lilmu'minīna wal-mu'mināti wa lā tazidiz-zalimīna illā tabārā

My Lord, forgive me and my parents and whoever enters my house a believer and the believing men and believing women. And do not increase the wrongdoers except in destruction.

Source: Quran (71:28)

GLORIFICATION & REMEMBRANCE OF ALLAH ﷻ

(19)

سُبْحانَ اللَّهِ وبِحَمْدِهِ، سُبْحانَ اللَّهِ العَظِيمِ

subhānallāhi wa bihamdihi subhānallāhil-'azīm

Glory is to Allah and all praise is to Him.
Glory is to Allah, The Great.

Source: al-Bukhari and Muslim

---

(20)

سُبْحَانَ اللهِ والحَمْدُ للهِ لَا إِلَهَ إِلَّا اللهُ واللهُ أَكْبَرُ

subhānallāhi wal-hamdullilāhi lā ilāha illallāhu wallāhu akbar

Glory is to Allah and praise is to Allah. There is no God (worthy of worship) but Allah and Allah is greater.

Source: Muslim

---

(21)

لَا إِلَهَ إِلَّا اللَّهُ وَحْدَهُ لَا شَرِيكَ لَهُ، لَهُ الْمُلْكُ وَلَهُ الْحَمْدُ، وَهُوَ عَلَى كُلِّ شَيْءٍ قَدِيرٌ

lā ilāha illallāhu wahdahu lā sharīka lah, lahul-mulk wa lahul-hamd, wa huwa 'alā kulli shay'in qadīr

There is no God (worthy of worship) but Allah alone, Who has no partners. To Him belongs the Dominion and to Him belongs all Praise and He is over all things competent.

Source: al-Bukhari

(22)

لا إِلَهَ إِلَّا اللَّهُ وَحْدَهُ لا شَرِيكَ له، اللَّهُ أَكْبَرُ كَبِيرًا، وَالْحَمْدُ لِلَّهِ كَثِيرًا، سُبْحَانَ اللهِ رَبِّ الْعَالَمِينَ، لا حَوْلَ وَلَا قُوَّةَ إِلَّا بِاللَّهِ الْعَزِيزِ الْحَكِيمِ

lā ilāha illallāhu wahdahu lā sharīka lah, allāhu akbaru kabīran wal-hamdullilahi kathīran subhānallāhi rabil-ʿalamīn wa lā hawla wa lā quwwata illā billāhil-ʿazīzil-hakīm

There is no God (worthy of worship) but Allah alone, Who has no partners. Allah is the Most Great and all praise is to Allah in abundance. Glory is to Allah, the Lord of the worlds. There is no power or might except with Allah, The Mighty and The Wise.

Source: Muslim

---

(23)

لَا إِلَهَ إِلَّا اللَّهُ الْعَظِيمُ الْحَلِيمُ لَا إِلَهَ إِلَّا اللَّهُ رَبُّ الْعَرْشِ الْعَظِيمِ لَا إِلَهَ إِلَّا اللَّهُ رَبُّ السَّمَوَاتِ، وَرَبُّ الأَرْضِ، وَرَبُّ الْعَرْشِ الْكَرِيمِ

lā ilāha illallahul-ʿazīmul-halīm, lā ilāha illallāhu rabbul-ʿarshil-azīm, lā ilāha illallāhu rabbus-samāwāt, wa rabbul-ard, wa rabbul-ʿarshil-karīm

There is no God (worthy of worship) but Allah, the Greatest and Forbearing. There is no God (worthy of worship) but Allah, the Lord of the Mighty Throne. There is no God (worthy of worship) but Allah, Lord of the heavens and Lord of the earth and Lord of the Supreme Throne.

Source: al-Bukhari

---

(24)

سُبْحَانَ اللهِ وَبِحَمْدِهِ، عَدَدَ خَلْقِهِ، وَرِضَا نَفْسِهِ، وَزِنَةَ عَرْشِهِ، وَمِدَادَ كَلِمَاتِهِ

subhānallāhi wa bihamdihi wa ʿaddada khalqihi wa ridā nafsihi wa zinata ʿarshihi wa midada kalimātih

Glory is to Allah and all praise is to Him, as many times as the number of His creatures, in accordance with His Good Pleasure, equal to the weight of His Throne and equal to the ink that may be used in recording the words (for His Praise).

Source: Muslim

---

(25)

اللَّهُمَّ أَنْتَ السَّلَامُ وَمِنْكَ السَّلَامُ، تَبَارَكْتَ ذَا الجَلَالِ وَالإِكْرَام

Allāhumma antas-salāmu wa minkas-salāmu tabārakta yā dhal-jalāli wal-i'krām

O Allah, You are the Grantor of peace, and peace comes from You. You are Blessing, O You Who have majesty and nobility.

Source: Muslim

---

(26)

اللَّهُمَّ أَعِنِّي على ذِكْرِكَ وشُكْرِكَ وحُسنِ عِبادَتِكَ

Allāhumma a'inī 'alā dhikrika wa shukrika wa husni 'ibādatik

O Allah, help me remember You, to be grateful to You and to worship You in an excellent manner.

Source: Abu Dawud

---

(27)

اللهم رَبَّنَا لَكَ الْحَمْدُ مِلْءَ السَّمَوَاتِ وَالأَرْضِ وَمِلْءَ مَا شِئْتَ مِنْ شَيْءٍ بَعْدُ أَهْلَ الثَّنَاءِ وَالْمَجْدِ أَحَقُّ مَا قَالَ الْعَبْدُ وَكُلُّنَا لَكَ عَبْدٌ اللَّهُمَّ لاَ مَانِعَ لِمَا أَعْطَيْتَ وَلاَ مُعْطِيَ لِمَا مَنَعْتَ وَلاَ يَنْفَعُ ذَا الْجَدِّ مِنْكَ الْجَدُّ

Allāhumma rabbanā lakal-hamd mila's-samāwāti wal-ardi wa mila' mā shi'ta min shayin b'adu ahluth-thanā' wal-majdi ahaqqu mā qālal-'abd, wa kullunā laka 'abd, Allāhumma lā mani'a limā 'ataita wa lā m'utiya limā man'ata wa lā yanfa'u dhal-jaddi minkal-jadd

O Allah, our Lord. To You belong all the praises that would fill the heavens and earth and the fullness of what You wish after that. To You belong all praise and grace. The most truthful words that (Your) slave can say and we are all Your slaves. O Allah, no one can deny to whom You give and no one can give to the one You deny. No fortune can be of benefit to its possessor against Allah's fortune.

Source: Muslim

---

(28)

وَأَنَا أَشْهَدُ أَنْ لاَ إِلَهَ إِلاَّ اللَّهُ وَحْدَهُ لاَ شَرِيكَ لَهُ وَأَنَّ مُحَمَّدًا عَبْدُهُ وَرَسُولُهُ رَضِيتُ بِاللَّهِ رَبًّا وَبِمُحَمَّدٍ رَسُولاً وَبِالإِسْلاَمِ دِينًا

Wa anā ashadu allā illāha illallāh wahdahu lā sharīka lah, wa anna muhammadan 'abdahu wa rasūluh, radītu billāhi rabbā, wa bi muhammadin rasūlā, wa bil-islāmi dīnā

I testify that there is no god (worthy of worship) but Allah Alone, He has no partners and that Muhammad ﷺ is His slave and Messenger. I am content with Allah as my Lord and with Mohammad as the Messenger and with Islam as my religion.

Source: al-Tirmidhi

(29)

قُلِ اللَّهُمَّ مَالِكَ الْمُلْكِ تُؤْتِي الْمُلْكَ مَن تَشَاءُ وَتَنزِعُ الْمُلْكَ مِمَّن تَشَاءُ وَتُعِزُّ مَن تَشَاءُ وَتُذِلُّ مَن تَشَاءُ بِيَدِكَ الْخَيْرُ إِنَّكَ عَلَى كُلِّ شَيْءٍ قَدِيرٌ
تُولِجُ اللَّيْلَ فِي النَّهَارِ وَتُولِجُ النَّهَارَ فِي اللَّيْلِ وَتُخْرِجُ الْحَيَّ مِنَ الْمَيِّتِ وَتُخْرِجُ الْمَيِّتَ مِنَ الْحَيِّ وَتَرْزُقُ مَن تَشَاءُ بِغَيْرِ حِسَابٍ

Allāhumma mālikal-mulki tu'til-mulka man tashau' wa tanzi'ul-mulka mimman tashau' wa tu'izzu man tashau' wa tudhillu man tashau' biyadikal-khayru innaka 'ala kulli shayi'n qadīr
Tūlijul-layla fin-nahari wa tūlijun-nahāra fil-layli wa tukhrijul-hayya minal-mayyiti wa tukhrijul-mayyita minal-hayyi wa tarzuqu man tashau' bighayri hisāb

O Allah, Owner of Sovereignty, You give sovereignty to whom You will and You take sovereignty away from whom You will. You honour whom You will and You humble whom You will. In Your hand is [all] good. Indeed, You are over all things competent.

You cause the night to enter the day, and You cause the day to enter the night and You bring the living out of the dead, and You bring the dead out of the living. And You give provision to whom You will without account.

Source: Quran (3:26-27)

---

(30)

رَبَّنَا إِنَّكَ تَعْلَمُ مَا نُخْفِي وَمَا نُعْلِنُ وَمَا يَخْفَىٰ عَلَى اللَّهِ مِن شَيْءٍ فِي الْأَرْضِ وَلَا فِي السَّمَاءِ

Rabbanā innaka ta'lamu mā nukhfī wa mā nu'lin, wa mā yakhfā 'alallāhi min shayi'n fil-ardi wa lā fis-samā'

Our Lord, indeed You know what we conceal and what we declare, and nothing is hidden from Allah on the earth or in the heaven.

Source: Quran (14:38)

---

(31)

حَسْبِيَ اللَّهُ لا إِلَـهَ إِلاَّ هُوَ عَلَيْهِ تَوَكَّلْتُ وَهُوَ رَبُّ الْعَرْشِ الْعَظِيمِ

hisbiyallāhu lā ilāha illa huwa 'alayhi tawakkaltu wa huwa rabbul-'arshil-'azīm

Sufficient for me is Allah. There is no deity except Him. On Him I have relied, and He is the Lord of the Great Throne.

Source: Quran (9:129)

SEEKING PROTECTION & RELIEF

(32)

لَا إِلَهَ إِلاَّ أَنْتَ سُبْحَانَكَ إِنِّي كُنْتُ مِنَ الظَّالِمِينَ

lā illāha illa anta subḥānaka innī kuntu minaz-zālimīn

There is no God (worthy of worship) but You. Glory be to You. Indeed I have been among the wrongdoers.

Source: Quran (21:87) / al-Tirmidhi

---

(33)

يَا حَيُّ يَا قَيُّومُ بِرَحْمَتِكَ أَسْتَغِيثُ

yā ḥayyu yā qayyūm, biraḥmatika astaghīth

O Ever Living, O Self-Sustaining Sustainer, by Your mercy I seek help.

Source: al-Tirmidhi

---

(34)

بِسْمِ اللَّهِ الَّذِي لَا يَضُرُّ مَعَ اسْمِهِ شَيْءٌ فِي الْأَرْضِ وَلَا فِي السَّمَاءِ وَهُوَ السَّمِيعُ الْعَلِيمُ

Bismillāhil-ladhī lā yaḍurru ma'as-mihi shayu'n fil-arḍi wa lā fis-samāi' wa huwas-samī'ul-'alīm

In the name of Allah with whose name nothing can be harmed on earth nor in the heavens and He is The All-Seeing, The All-Knowing.

Source: Sunan al-Tirmidhi

(35)

بِاللَّهِ مِنَ الْفِتَنِ مَا ظَهَرَ مِنْهَا وَمَا بَطَنَ أَعُوذُ

a'ūdhu billāhi minal-fitan, mā zahara minhā wa mā batan

I seek refuge in Allah from trials (or turmoil), whatever is visible of it and whatever is hidden of it.

Source: Muslim

---

(36)

اللَّهُمَّ إِنِّي أَعُوذُ بِكَ مِنْ زَوَالِ نِعْمَتِكَ، وَتَحَوُّلِ عَافِيَتِكَ، وَفُجَاءَةِ نِقْمَتِكَ، وَجَمِيعِ سَخَطِكَ

Allāhumma innī a'ūdhu bika min zawāli ni'matika wa tahawwuli 'āfiyatika wa fujāa'ti niqmatika wa jamī'i sakhatik

O Allah, I seek refuge in You from the deprivation of Your blessing and from losing Your protection and from Your sudden wrath and from every displeasure of Yours.

Source: Muslim

---

(37)

اللَّهُمَّ إِنِّي أَعُوذُ بِكَ مِنْ شَرِّ مَا عَمِلْتُ وَمِنْ شَرِّ مَا لَمْ أَعْمَلْ

Allāhumma innī a'ūdhu bika min sharri mā 'amilatu wa min sharri mā lam 'amal

O Allah, I seek refuge in You from the evils of what I have done and from the evil of what I have not done.

Source: Muslim

---

(38)

اللَّهُمَّ إِنِّي أَعُوذُ بِكَ مِنْ شَرِّ سَمْعِي، وَمِنْ شَرِّ بَصَرِي، وَمِنْ شَرِّ لِسَانِي، وَمِنْ شَرِّ قَلْبِي

Allāhumma innī a'ūdhu bika min sharri sam'ī wa min sharri basarī wa min sharri lissānī wa min sharri qalbī

O Allah, I seek refuge in you from the evils of my hearing and from the evils of my sight and from the evils of my tongue and from the evils of my heart.

Source: al-Tirmidhi

---

(39)

أعوذُ باللهِ السَّـميعِ العَليمِ مِنَ الشَّيطانِ الرَّجيمِ، مِن هَمْزِه ونَفخِه ونَفثِه

A'ūdhu billāhis-samī'il-'alīm, minash-shaitānir- rajīm, min hamzihi, wa nafkhihi, wa-nafthih

I seek refuge in Allah The All-Hearer and The All-Knower, from the evil (cursed) Satan and his whispers (temptations), his blowing and his breath (spits).

Source: Abu-Dawud

---

(40)

أَعُوذُ بِكَلِـمَاتِ اللهِ التَّامَّاتِ مِن شَرِّ ما خَلَقَ

A'ūdhu bi-kalimātillāhit-tāmāti min sharri mā khalaq

I seek refuge in Allah's complete (and perfect) words from the evils of what He has created.

Source: Muslim

---

(41)

اللَّهُمَّ إِنِّي أَعُوذُ بِكَ مِن فِتْنَةِ النَّارِ وعَذابِ النَّارِ، وفِتْنَةِ القَبْرِ وعَذابِ القَبْرِ، وشَرِّ فِتْنَةِ الغِنَى وشَرِّ فِتْنَةِ الفَقْرِ

Allāhumma innī a'ūdhu bika min fitnatin-nār, wa-'adhābin-nār, wa-fitnatil-qabr, wa-'adhābil-qabr, wa sharrī fitnatil-ghinā, wa sharrī fitnatil-faqr

O Allah, I seek refuge in You from the trials (fitnah) of the Hell Fire and the punishment of the Hell Fire, and from the trials of the grave and the punishment of the grave, and from the trials of abundance and from the trials of poverty.

Source: al-Bukhari

(42)

اللَّهُمَّ إِنِّي أَعُوذُ بِكَ مِن عَذَابِ جَهَنَّمَ، وَمِنْ عَذَابِ الْقَبْرِ، وَمِنْ فِتْنَةِ الْمَحْيَا وَالْمَمَاتِ، وَمِنْ شَرِّ فِتْنَةِ الْمَسِيحِ الدَّجَّالِ

Allāhumma innī aʿūdhu bika min ʿadhābi jahannam, wa min ʿadhābil-qabr, wa-min fitnatil-mahyā wal-mamāt, wa min sharri fitnatil-masīhid-dajjāl

O Allah, I seek refuge in You from the punishment of Hell and from the punishment of the grave and from the trials of this life and death and from the trials of the al-Masih al-Dajjal (the False Messiah)

Source: al-Bukhari

---

(43)

اللَّهُمَّ أَعُوذُ بِرِضَاكَ مِن سَخَطِكَ، وَبِمُعَافَاتِكَ مِن عُقُوبَتِكَ، وَأَعُوذُ بِكَ مِنْكَ لَا أُحْصِي ثَنَاءً عَلَيْكَ أَنْتَ كَمَا أَثْنَيْتَ عَلَى نَفْسِكَ

Allāhumma aʿūdhu biridāka min sakhatik, wa bimuʿāfātika min ʿuqūbatik, wa aʿūdhu bika mink, lā uhsī thanāaʾn ʿalayka anta kamā athnayta ʿalā nafsik

O Allah, I seek refuge in Your satisfaction (pleasure) from Your anger, and in Your forgiveness from Your punishment, and in You from You. I cannot enumerate Your praises as You praise Yourself.

Source: Muslim

---

(44)

اللَّهُمَّ رَحْمَتَكَ أَرْجُو فَلَا تَكِلْنِي إِلَى نَفْسِي طَرْفَةَ عَيْنٍ، وَأَصْلِحْ لِي شَأْنِي كُلَّهُ، لَا إِلَهَ إِلَّا أَنْتَ

Allāhumma rahmataka arjū falā takilnī ilā nafsī tarfata ʿayn, wa aslihlī shaʾnī kullahu lā ilāha illā ant

O Allah, I hope for Your mercy. So don't let me be in charge of myself (my affairs) even for the wink of an eye and resolve all my affairs. There is no God (worthy of worship) but You.

Source: Abu-Dawud

(45)

اللَّهُمَّ إِنِّي أَعُوذُ بِعِزَّتِكَ -لَا إِلَهَ إِلَّا أَنْتَ- أَنْ تُضِلَّنِي، أَنْتَ الْحَيُّ الَّذِي لَا يَمُوتُ، وَالْجِنُّ وَالْإِنْسُ يَمُوتُونَ

Allāhumma innī a'ūdhu bi'izzatikal-ladhī lā ilāha illā ant, alladhī lā yamūt, wal-jinnu wal-insu yamūtūn

O Allah, I seek refuge in You by Your honor for there is no God (worthy of worship) but You, the One who doesn't die while the Jinn and the human beings die.

Source: al-Bukhari

---

(46)

اللَّهُمَّ لَا سَهْلَ إِلَّا مَا جَعَلْتَهُ سَهْلًا، وَأَنْتَ تَجْعَلُ الْحَزْنَ إِذَا شِئْتَ سَهْلًا

Allāhumma lā sahla illā mā ja'altahu sahlā, wa anta taj'alul-hazna idhā shi'ta sahlā

O Allah, There is no ease except that which You make easy, and if you want, You can make grief and difficulties easy.

Source: Ibn Hibbān

---

(47)

اللَّهُ لَا إِلَهَ إِلَّا هُوَ الْحَيُّ الْقَيُّومُ لَا تَأْخُذُهُ سِنَةٌ وَلَا نَوْمٌ لَهُ مَا فِي السَّمَاوَاتِ وَمَا فِي الْأَرْضِ مَنْ ذَا الَّذِي يَشْفَعُ عِنْدَهُ إِلَّا بِإِذْنِهِ يَعْلَمُ مَا بَيْنَ أَيْدِيهِمْ وَمَا خَلْفَهُمْ وَلَا يُحِيطُونَ بِشَيْءٍ مِنْ عِلْمِهِ إِلَّا بِمَا شَاءَ وَسِعَ كُرْسِيُّهُ السَّمَاوَاتِ وَالْأَرْضَ وَلَا يَئُودُهُ حِفْظُهُمَا وَهُوَ الْعَلِيُّ الْعَظِيمُ

Allāhu lā ilāha illā huwal-hayyul-qayyūmu la ta'khudhuhu sinatun wa lā nawm, lahu mā fis-samāwāti wa ma fil-ardi man dhā-ladhī yashfa'u 'indahu illā bi-ithnih, y'alamu mā bayna aydīhim wa mā khalfahum, walā yuhītūna bishay'in min 'ilmihi illā bimā shā' wasi'a kursiyyuhus-samāwāti wal-ard, wa lā yauduhu hifzuhumā wa huwal-'aliyyul-'azīm

Allah - there is no deity except Him, the Ever-Living, the Sustainer of [all] existence. Neither drowsiness overtakes Him nor sleep. To Him belongs whatever is in the heavens and whatever is on the earth. Who is it that can intercede with

Him except by His permission? He knows what is [presently] before them and what will be after them, and they encompass not a thing of His knowledge except for what He wills. His Kursi extends over the heavens and the earth, and their preservation tires Him not. And He is the Most High, the Most Great.

Source: Quran (2:255)

---

(48)

رَبَّنَا لَا تُؤَاخِذْنَا إِن نَّسِينَا أَوْ أَخْطَأْنَا رَبَّنَا وَلَا تَحْمِلْ عَلَيْنَا إِصْرًا كَمَا حَمَلْتَهُ عَلَى الَّذِينَ مِن قَبْلِنَا رَبَّنَا وَلَا تُحَمِّلْنَا مَا لَا طَاقَةَ لَنَا بِهِ وَاعْفُ عَنَّا وَاغْفِرْ لَنَا وَارْحَمْنَا أَنتَ مَوْلَانَا فَانصُرْنَا عَلَى الْقَوْمِ الْكَافِرِينَ

Rabbanā la tuākhidhnā in nasīnā aw akhta'nā rabbanā walā tahmil 'alaynā isran kamā hamaltahu 'alal-a'dhīna min qablinā rabbanā wa lā tuhammilnā mā lā tāqata lanā bihi w'afu 'annā waghfir lanā warhamnā anta mawlānā fansurnā 'alal-qawmil-kāfirīn

Our Lord, do not impose blame upon us if we have forgotten or erred. Our Lord, and lay not upon us a burden like that which You laid upon those before us. Our Lord, and burden us not with that which we have no ability to bear. And pardon us and forgive us and have mercy upon us. You are our protector, so give us victory over the disbelieving people.

Source: Quran (2:286)

---

(49)

رَبِّ إِنِّي أَعُوذُ بِكَ أَنْ أَسْأَلَكَ مَا لَيْسَ لِي بِهِ عِلْمٌ وَإِلَّا تَغْفِرْ لِي وَتَرْحَمْنِي أَكُن مِّنَ الْخَاسِرِينَ

Rabbi innī a'ūthubika an asalaka mā laysa lī bihi 'ilm, wa illa taghfirlī wa tarhamnī akum-minal-khāsirīn

My Lord, I seek refuge in You from asking that of which I have no knowledge. And unless You forgive me and have mercy upon me, I will be among the losers.

Source: Quran (11:47)

(50)

رَبِّ أَعُوذُ بِكَ مِنْ هَمَزَاتِ الشَّيَاطِينِ وَأَعُوذُ بِكَ رَبِّ أَنْ يَحْضُرُونِ

Rabbi a'ūthu bika min hamazātish-shayātīn

Wa a'ūthu bika rabbi an yahdurūn

My Lord, I seek refuge in You from the incitements of the devils,
And I seek refuge in You, my Lord, lest they be present with me.

Source: Quran (23:97-98)

---

(51)

رَبَّنَا اصْرِفْ عَنَّا عَذَابَ جَهَنَّمَ إِنَّ عَذَابَهَا كَانَ غَرَامًا

Rabbanasrif 'annā 'athāba jahannam, inna 'athābahā kāna gharāmā

Our Lord, avert from us the punishment of Hell. Indeed, its
punishment is ever adhering.

Source: Quran (25:65)

---

(52)

مِنْ جَهْدِ الْبَلَاءِ وَدَرَكِ الشَّقَاءِ وَسُوءِ الْقَضَاءِ وَشَمَاتَةِ الْأَعْدَاءِ اللهم إني أعوذ بك

Allāhumma innī a'ūdhu bika min jahdil-balā', wa darakish-shaqqā', wa sūiqqadā', wa shamātatil-'adā'

O Allah, I seek refuge in You from the strongest affliction, from
the burden of hardships (and worries), from bad judgments and
from the enemy's malicious rejoicing (for my sufferings).

Source: al-Bukhari

---

(53)

اللَّهُمَّ إِنِّي أَسْأَلُكَ الْعَافِيَةَ فِي الدُّنْيَا وَالْآخِرَةِ اللَّهُمَّ إِنِّي أَسْأَلُكَ الْعَفْوَ وَالْعَافِيَةَ فِي دِينِي وَدُنْيَايَ وَأَهْلِي وَمَالِي اللَّهُمَّ اسْتُرْ عَوْرَتِي وَآمِنْ رَوْعَاتِي اللَّهُمَّ احْفَظْنِي مِنْ بَيْنِ يَدَيَّ وَمِنْ خَلْفِي وَعَنْ يَمِينِي وَعَنْ شِمَالِي وَمِنْ فَوْقِي وَأَعُوذُ بِعَظَمَتِكَ أَنْ أُغْتَالَ مِنْ تَحْتِي

Allāhumma innī asalukal-'āfiyata fid-dunyā wal-ākhirah,

*Allāhumma innī asalukal-'afwa wal-'āfiyata fī dīnī wa dunyāya
wa ahlī wa mālī, Allāhummastur 'awrātī wa i āmin raw'ātī,*

Allāhummahfaznī min bayni yadayya, wa min khalfī, wa 'an

*yamīnī wa 'an shimālī, wa min fawqī, wa a'ūdhu bi'azamatika
an aghtāla min tahtī*

O Allah, I ask You for security in this world and in the Hereafter. O Allah, I ask You for pardon and security in my religion and my worldly affairs, in my family and my wealth. O Allah, conceal my faults and keep me safe from the things I fear. O Allah, protect me from the front and the back, from my right and my left and from above, and I seek refuge in Your Greatness from being swallowed from beneath (facing a great loss).

Source: Abu-Dawud

---

(54)

اللَّهُمَّ إِنِّي أَعُوذُ بِكَ مِنَ الْكَسَلِ وَالْهَرَمِ وَالْمَأْثَمِ وَالْمَغْرَمِ

Allāhumma innī a'ūdhu bika minal-kasal, wal-haram, wal-ma'thami wal-maghram

O Allah, I seek refuge in You from laziness and old age, and transgressions (sins) and debt (loss and damages).

Source: al-Bukhari

---

(55)

اللَّهُمَّ إِنِّي أَعُوذُ بِكَ مِنَ الْهَمِّ وَالْحَزَنِ وَضَلَعِ الدَّيْنِ وَغَلَبَةِ الرِّجَالِ

Allāhumma innī a'ūdhu bika minal-hammi wal-hazani wa dal'id-dayni wa ghalabatir-rijāl

O Allah, I seek refuge in You from grief and anxiety, from the hardships of debt, and from being overpowered by men.

Source: Abu Dawood

---

(56)

اللَّهُمَّ إِنِّي أَعُوذُ بِكَ مِنَ العَجْزِ وَالكَسَلِ، وَالجُبْنِ وَالهَرَمِ،
وَأَعُوذُ بِكَ مِن فِتْنَةِ المَحْيَا وَالمَمَاتِ

Allāhumma innī a'ūdhu bika minal-'ajzi wal-kasal, wal-jubni wal-bukhl, wa-aʿūdhu bika min ʿadhabil-qabr, wa-aʿūdhu bika min fitantil-mahyā wal-mamāt

O Allah, I ask for Your protection from incapability (giving up) and laziness, from cowardice and stinginess, and I ask for Your protection from the punishment of the grave, and I ask for Your protection from the trials (and challenges) of life and death.

Source: al-Bukhari

---

(57)

اللهم إني أعوذ بك من منكرات الأخلاق والاعمال والاهواء

Allāhumma innī aʿūdhu bika min munkarātil-akhlāq, wal-ʿamāli wal-ahwāʾ

O Allah, I seek refuge in You from evil manners (and character), deeds and desires.

Source: al-Tirmidhi

---

(58)

اللَّهُمَّ إِنِّي أَعُوذُ بِكَ مِنَ الجوعِ فإِنَّهُ بئسَ الضَّجيعُ وأعوذُ بِكَ مِنَ الخيانةِ فإنَّها بئستِ البطانةُ

Allāhumma innī aʿūdhu bika minal-jūʿ, faʾinnahu biʾsad-dajīʿ, wa aʿūdhu bika minal-khiyānah fa innahā biʾsatil-biṭānah

O Allah, I seek refuge in You from hunger because it is the worst ally and I seek refuge in You from betrayal because it is the worst mate.

Source: Abu-Dawud

---

(59)

اللَّهُمَّ إِنِّي أَعُوذُ بِكَ مِنَ الْهَدْمِ وَأَعُوذُ بِكَ مِنَ التَّرَدِّي وَأَعُوذُ بِكَ مِنَ الْغَرَقِ وَالْحَرَقِ وَالْهَرَمِ وَأَعُوذُ بِكَ أَنْ يَتَخَبَّطَنِي الشَّيْطَانُ عِنْدَ الْمَوْتِ

Allāhumma innī aʿūdhu bika minal-hadmi wa aʿūdhu bika minat-taraddī wa aʿūdhu bika minal-gharaqi wal-ḥarqi wal-harami wa a'ūdhu bika min an yatakhabbataniyash- shaytānu 'indal-mawt

O Allah, I seek refuge in You from demolitions and I seek refuge in You from falling from heights and I seek refuge in You from drowning, burning and old age. I seek refuge in You from Satan's temptations (and misguidance) at death.

Source: Abu-Dawud

---

(60)

اللَّهُمَّ رَبَّ السَّمَوَاتِ وَرَبَّ الْأَرْضِ وَرَبَّ الْعَرْشِ الْعَظِيمِ رَبَّنَا وَرَبَّ كُلِّ شَيْءٍ فَالِقَ الْحَبِّ وَالنَّوَى وَمُنْزِلَ التَّوْرَاةِ وَالْإِنْجِيلِ وَالْفُرْقَانِ أَعُوذُ بِكَ مِنْ شَرِّ كُلِّ شَيْءٍ أَنْتَ آخِذٌ بِنَاصِيَتِهِ اللَّهُمَّ أَنْتَ الْأَوَّلُ فَلَيْسَ قَبْلَكَ شَيْءٌ وَأَنْتَ الْآخِرُ فَلَيْسَ بَعْدَكَ شَيْءٌ وَأَنْتَ الظَّاهِرُ فَلَيْسَ فَوْقَكَ شَيْءٌ وَأَنْتَ الْبَاطِنُ فَلَيْسَ دُونَكَ شَيْءٌ اقْضِ عَنَّا الدَّيْنَ وَأَغْنِنَا مِنَ الْفَقْرِ

Allāhumma rabbas-samāwāti wa rabbal-ardi wa rabbal-'arshil-'azīm, rabbanā wa rabba kulli shayi'n fāliqal-habbi wan-nawā wa munzilat-tawrāti wal-injīli wal-furqān, a'ūdu bika min sharri kulli shayi'n anta ākhidhun bināsiyatih, Allāhumma antal-awwalu falaysa qablaka shayu'n, wa antal-ākhiru falaysa b'adaka shayu'n wa antaz-zāhiru falaysa fawqaka shayu'n wa antal-bātinu falaysa dūnnaka shayu'n iqdi 'annad-dayna wa aghninā minal-faqr

O Allah, Lord of the heavens and the earth and Lord of the Great Throne. Our Lord and Lord of all things, the Splitter of the seed grain and date stone and the Revealer of the Torah and the Bible and the Quran. I seek refuge in You from the evil of all things, which You hold under Your control. O Allah, You are the First, there was nothing before You. You are the Last, and there's nothing after You. You are the Manifest, and there's nothing above You. You are the Concealed, and there's nothing beyond You. Remove the burden of our debt and relieve us from poverty.

Source: Muslim

(61)

اللَّهُمَّ أَصْلِحْ لِي دِينِي الَّذِي هُوَ عِصْمَةُ أَمْرِي، وَأَصْلِحْ لِي دُنْيَايَ الَّتِي فِيهَا مَعَاشِي، وَأَصْلِحْ لِي آخِرَتِي الَّتِي فِيهَا مَعَادِي، وَاجْعَلِ الحَيَاةَ زِيَادَةً لِي فِي كُلِّ خَيْرٍ، وَاجْعَلِ المَوْتَ رَاحَةً لِي مِن كُلِّ شَرٍّ

Allāhumma aslih lī dīnī alladhī huwa 'ismatu amrī wa aslih lī dunyāyallatī fīhā ma'āshī, wa aslih lī ākhiratīllatī fīha ma'ādī, waj'alil-hayāta ziyādatal-lī fī kulli khayr, waj'alil-mawta rāhatal-lī min kulli sharr

O Allah, set right for me my religion which is the safeguard of my affairs, and set right for me my worldly life that is the place of my living, and set right for me my hereafter to which is my return, and make my life abundant with goodness, and cause my death to bring me comfort from all evils (trials and challenges).

Source: Muslim

---

(62)

اللَّهُمَّ اقْسِمْ لَنَا مِنْ خَشْيَتِكَ مَا تَحُولُ بِهِ بَيْنَنَا وَبَيْنَ مَعَاصِيكَ، وَمِنْ طَاعَتِكَ مَا تُبَلِّغُنَا بِهِ جَنَّتَكَ، وَمِنَ الْيَقِينِ مَا تُهَوِّنُ بِهِ عَلَيْنَا مَصَائِبَ الدُّنْيَا، اللَّهُمَّ مَتِّعْنَا بِأَسْمَاعِنَا، وَأَبْصَارِنَا، وَقُوَّاتِنَا مَا أَحْيَيْتَنَا، وَاجْعَلْهُ الْوَارِثَ مِنَّا، وَاجْعَلْ ثَأْرَنَا عَلَى مَنْ ظَلَمَنَا، وَانْصُرْنَا عَلَى مَنْ عَادَانَا، وَلَا تَجْعَلْ مُصِيبَتَنَا فِي دِينِنَا، وَلَا تَجْعَلِ الدُّنْيَا أَكْبَرَ هَمِّنَا، وَلَا مَبْلَغَ عِلْمِنَا، وَلَا تُسَلِّطْ عَلَيْنَا مَنْ لَا يَرْحَمُنَا.

Allāhummaqsim lanā min khashyatika mā yahūlu baynanā wa bayna ma'āsīk, wa min tā'atika mā tuballighunā bihi jannatak, wa minal-yaqīni mā tuhawwinu bihi 'alaynā musībātid-dunyā, wa matti'nā bi-asmā'inā, wa absārina, wa quwwatinā mā ahyaytanā, waj'allhul-wāritha minnā, wa-j'al thā'ranā 'alā man zalamanā wansurnā alā man 'ādānā, wa lā taj'al musībatana fī dīninā wa lā taj'alid-dunyā akbara hamminā wa lā mablagha 'ilminā wa lā tusallit 'alaynā mal-lā yarhamunā

O Allah, apportion for us a fear of You that will come between us and disobedience of You and (apportion for us) obedience to You, which will lead us to Your paradise (Jannah). And (apportion for us) certainty in faith that will ease our hardships in this life. And (apportion for us) enjoyment of our hearing, sight, and energy for as long as You grant us life, and until our death. O Allah, let our revenge fall upon those who have wronged us, and grant us victory over those who have declared enmity against us, and do not make our difficulties in our religion, and do not make this worldly life a big concern for us nor the limit of our knowledge, and don't give control over us to those who are not merciful to us.

Source: al-Tirmidhi

---

(63)

اللّهُمَّ فاطِرَ السَّماواتِ والأرضِ عالِمَ الغيبِ والشَّهادةِ رَبَّ كلِّ شيءٍ ومليكَهُ ومالِكَهُ
أشهدُ أن لا إلهَ إلَّا أنتَ أعوذُ بكَ من شرِّ نفسي ومن شرِّ الشَّيطانِ وشركِهِ

Allāhumma ʿālimal-ghaibi wash-shahāda fāṭiras-samāwāti wal-arḍ, rabba kuli shay'in wa malīkah, ash-hadu allā ilāha illa ant, aʿūdhu bika min sharri nafsī, wa min sharrish-shayṭāni wa shirkih

O Allah, Knower of the Unseen and Seen, Creator of the heavens and the earth, Lord of everything and its Owner. I testify that there's no God (worthy of worship) but You. I seek refuge in You from the evils of myself and from the evils of Satan and his shirk.

Source: al-Tirmidhi

---

(64)

اللّهُمَّ قِنِي عذابَكَ يومَ تبعَثُ عبادَكَ

Allāhumma qinī ʿadhābaka yawma tabʿathu ʿibādak

O Allah, keep me away from Your punishment on the day when You resurrect Your slaves.

Source: Abu-Dawud

(65)

اللَّهُمَّ إِنِّي أَعُوذُ بِكَ مِنَ العَجْزِ وَالْكَسَلِ، وَالْجُبْنِ وَالْبُخْلِ، وَالْهَرَمِ، وَعَذَابِ القَبْرِ، اللَّهُمَّ آتِ نَفْسِي تَقْوَاهَا، وَزَكِّهَا أَنْتَ خَيْرُ مَنْ زَكَّاهَا، أَنْتَ وَلِيُّهَا وَمَوْلَاهَا، اللَّهُمَّ إِنِّي أَعُوذُ بِكَ مِنْ عِلْمٍ لَا يَنْفَعُ، وَمِنْ قَلْبٍ لَا يَخْشَعُ، وَمِنْ نَفْسٍ لَا تَشْبَعُ، وَمِنْ دَعْوَةٍ لَا يُسْتَجَابُ لَهَا

Allāhumma āati nafsī taqwāhā wa zakkihā anta khayru man zakkāhā, anta waliyyuhā wa mawlāhā, Allāhumma innī a'ūdhu bika min 'ilmil-lā yanfa'u wa min qalbil-lā yakhsha'u wa min nafsil-lā tashba'u wa min d'awatil-lā yustajābu lahā

O Allah, grant my soul its devoutness (God consciousness) and purify it for You are the best to purify it. You are its Guardian and Lord. O Allah, I seek refuge in You from knowledge that isn't beneficial and from a heart that's not fearful (of You) and from a soul that doesn't feel contented and from a supplication that doesn't get answered.

Source: Muslim

---

(66)

اللَّهُمَّ إِنِّي أَعُوذُ بِكَ أَنْ أُشْرِكَ بِكَ وَأَنَا أَعْلَمُ، وَأَسْتَغْفِرُكَ لِمَا لَا أَعْلَمُ

Allāhumma innī a'ūdhu bika min an ushrika bika shaya'n 'alamuhu wa astaghfiruka limā lā 'alam

O Allah, I seek refuge in You from knowingly associating partners with You, and I ask for Your forgiveness when I do so and am not aware of it.

Source: Ahmad

---

(67)

رَبِّ اشْرَحْ لِي صَدْرِي
وَيَسِّرْ لِي أَمْرِي
وَاحْلُلْ عُقْدَةً مِّن لِّسَانِي
يَفْقَهُوا قَوْلِي

Rabbish-shrahlī sadrī
Wa yassirlī amrī
Wahlul-'uqdatam mil-lisānī

Yafqahu qawlī
My Lord, expand for me my breast [with assurance]
And ease for me my task
And untie the knot from my tongue
That they may understand my speech

Source: Quran (20:25-28)

---

(68)

رَبِّ انصُرْنِي عَلَى الْقَوْمِ الْمُفْسِدِينَ

Rabbinsurnī ʿalal-qawmil-mufsidīn
My Lord, support me against the corrupting people.

Source: Quran (29:30)

SEEKING GUIDANCE, BENEFIT & BLESSINGS

(69)
اللَّهُمَّ مُصَرِّفَ القُلُوبِ صَرِّفْ قُلُوبَنَا عَلَى طَاعَتِكَ

Allāhumma musarrifal-qulūb sarrif qulūbunā 'alā tā'atik

Oh Changer of Hearts, direct our hearts towards your obedience.

Source: Muslim

---

(70)
يَا مُقَلِّبَ الْقُلُوبِ ثَبِّتْ قَلْبِي عَلَى دِينِكَ

Yā muqallibal-qulūbi thab-bit qalbī 'alā dīnik

Oh Turner of the Hearts, fixate my heart upon your religion.

Source: al-Tirmidhi

---

(71)
اللَّهُمَّ ثَبِّتْنِي وَاجْعَلْنِي هَادِياً مَهْدِيّاً

Allāhumma thabbitnī waj'alnī hādiyam-mahdiyyā

O Allah, make me steadfast (in faith), make me guided and a means of guidance.

Source: al-Bukhari

---

(72)
اللَّهُمَّ إِنِّي أَسْأَلُكَ حُبَّكَ وَحُبَّ مَنْ يُحِبُّكَ وَالْعَمَلَ الَّذِي يُبَلِّغُنِي حُبَّكَ اللَّهُمَّ اجْعَلْ حُبَّكَ أَحَبَّ إِلَيَّ مِنْ نَفْسِي وَأَهْلِي وَمِنَ الْمَاءِ الْبَارِدِ

*Allāhumma innī asaluka hubbaka wa hubba man yuhibbuk,
wal-'amalal-ladhī yuballighunī hubbak, Allāhummaj'al hubbaka
ahabba ilayya min nafsī wa ahlī wa minal-māi'l-bārid*

O Allah, indeed, I ask You for Your love and the love of those
who love You, and the deeds that will bring me closer to
Your love. O Allah, make Your love more beloved to me than
myself, my family and cold water.

Source: al-Tirmidhi

---

(73)

اللَّهُمَّ ارْزُقْنِي حُبَّكَ، وحُبَّ مَنْ يَنْفَعُنِي حُبُّهُ عِنْدَكَ، اللَّهُمَّ مَا رَزَقْتَنِي مِمَّا أُحِبُّ فَاجْعَلْهُ
قُوَّةً لِي فِيمَا تُحِبُّ، اللَّهُمَّ مَا زَوَيْتَ عَنِّي مِمَّا أُحِبُّ فَاجْعَلْهُ فَرَاغاً لِي فِيمَا تُحِبُّ

*Allāhummar-zuqnī hubbaka wa hubba man yanfa'unī 'indak,
Allāhumma mā razaqtanī mimmā u'hibbu faj'alhu quwwatan
lī fīmā tuhibb, Allāhumma mā zawayta 'annī mimmā u'hibbu
faj'alhu farāghan lī fīmā tuhibb*

Oh Allah, sustain me with Your love and with the love of
those whose love benefits me with You. Oh Allah, whatever You have given me of the things that I love make them
a strong means for me to do the things that You love. Oh
Allah, in whatever You have removed from me of what I love,
continue in distancing it from me toward what You love.

Source: al-Tirmidhi

---

(74)

اللَّهُمَّ إِنِّي أَسْأَلُكَ الْهُدَى وَالتُّقَى، وَالْعَفَافَ وَالْغِنَى

Allāhumma innī asalukal-hudā wat-tuqā wal-'afāfa wal-ghinā

O Allah, I ask You of guidance, devoutness (piety), chastity
(virtuousness) and abundance (in provisions).

Source: Muslim

(75)

رَبَّنَا آمَنَّا بِمَا أَنزَلْتَ وَاتَّبَعْنَا الرَّسُولَ فَاكْتُبْنَا مَعَ الشَّاهِدِينَ

Rabbanā āmannā faktubnā ma'ash-shāhidīn

Our Lord, we have believed, so register us
among the witnesses.

Source: Quran (5:83)

---

(76)

رَبِّ اجْعَلْنِي مُقِيمَ الصَّلَاةِ وَمِن ذُرِّيَّتِي رَبَّنَا وَتَقَبَّلْ دُعَاءِ

*Rabbij'alnī muqīmas-salāti wa min dhurriyyatī
rabbanā wa taqabbal du'ā*

My Lord, make me an establisher of prayer, and [many] from
my descendants. Our Lord, and accept my supplication.

Source: Quran (14:40)

---

(77)

رَبَّنَا أَفْرِغْ عَلَيْنَا صَبْرًا وَتَوَفَّنَا مُسْلِمِينَ

Rabbanā afrigh 'alaynā sabran watawaf-fanā muslimīn

Our Lord, pour upon us patience and let us die as Muslims
[in submission to You].

Source: Quran (7:126)

---

(78)

رَبِّ أَوْزِعْنِي أَنْ أَشْكُرَ نِعْمَتَكَ الَّتِي أَنْعَمْتَ عَلَيَّ وَعَلَىٰ وَالِدَيَّ وَأَنْ أَعْمَلَ صَالِحًا تَرْضَاهُ وَأَدْخِلْنِي بِرَحْمَتِكَ فِي عِبَادِكَ الصَّالِحِينَ

*Rabbi awz'inī an ashkura n'imatakal-latī an'amta 'alayya wa
'alā wālidayya wa an a'amala sālihan tardahu wa adkhilnī
birahmatika fī 'ibādikas-sālihīn*

My Lord, enable me to be grateful for Your favour
which You have bestowed upon me and upon my
parents and to do righteousness of which You approve.
And admit me by Your mercy into [the ranks of] Your

righteous servants.

Source: Quran (27:19)

---

(79)

اللَّهُمَّ اغْفِرْ لِي وَارْحَمْنِي وَعَافِنِي وَاهْدِنِي وَارْزُقْنِي

Allāhummaghfir lī warhamnī wahdinī, wa 'āfinī waruzuqnī

O Allah, forgive me and have mercy on me. Guide me, grant me health (and security), and provide me with sustenance.

Source: Muslim

---

(80)

اللَّهُمَّ اغْفِرْ لِي ذَنْبِي ، وَوَسِّعْ لِي فِي دَارِي ، وَبَارِكْ لِي فِيمَا رَزَقْتَنِي

*Allāhumma-ghfir lī dhanbī wa wass'i lī fī dārī,
wa bārik lī fīmā razaqtanī*

O Allah, forgive me my sins and expand my dwelling (living), and bless whatever You provide me.

Source: al-Tirmidhi

---

(81)

رَبَّنَا آتِنَا مِنْ لَدُنْكَ رَحْمَةً وَهَيِّئْ لَنَا مِنْ أَمْرِنَا رَشَدًا

*Rabbanā ātinā mil-ladunka rahmatan wa hayyilanā
min amrinā rashadā*

Our Lord, grant us from Yourself mercy and prepare for us from our affair right guidance.

Source: Quran (18:10)

---

(82)

اللَّهُمَّ اكْفِنِي بِحَلَالِكَ عَنْ حَرَامِكَ، وَأَغْنِنِي بِفَضْلِكَ عَمَّنْ سِوَاكَ

*Allāhumma-akfinī bihalālika 'an harāmika wa aghninī
bifadlika 'amman siwāk*

O Allah, suffice me (grant me) with that which is lawful to

You rather than unlawful to You, and enrich me with Your Grace (and favours) so that I am not in need of anyone else.

Source: al-Tirmidhi

---

(83)

اللَّهُمَّ أَكْثِرْ مَالِي، وَوَلَدِي، وَبَارِكْ لِي فِيمَا أَعْطَيْتَنِي
اللَّهُمَّ عافِني في بـدَنـي اللَّهُمَّ عافِني في سَـمعي اللَّهُمَّ عافِني في بَصَري لا إلَه إلَّا أنتَ

*Allāhumma 'āfini fī badanī, Allāhumma 'āfini fī sam'ī,
Allāhumma 'āfini fī basarī, lā illāha illā ant*

O Allah, grant me a healthy body. O Allah, grant me healthy hearing. O Allah, grant me healthy eyesight. There is no God (worthy of worship) but You.

Source: Abu-Dawud

---

(84)

اللَّهُـمَّ رَبَّ جِبْرَائِيلَ، وَمِيكَائِيلَ، وإسْرَافِيلَ، فَاطِرَ السَّمَوَاتِ وَالأرض، عَالِمَ الغَيْبِ وَالشَّـهَادَةِ، أَنْـتَ تَحْكُمُ بَيْنَ عِبَادِكَ فِيمَا كَانُوا فِيهِ يَخْتَلِفُونَ، اهْدِني لِما اخْتُلِفَ فيه مِنَ الحَقِّ بِإِذْنِكَ؛ إِنَّكَ تَهْدِي مَنْ تَشَاءُ إِلى صِرَاطٍ مُسْتَقِيمٍ

Allāhumma rabba jibrāila wa mīkāila wa isrāfila fātiras-samāwāti wal-ard, 'ālimal-ghaibi wash-shahādati, anta tahkumu bayna 'ibādika fīmā kānū fīhi yakhtalifūn, ihdinī limakhtulifa fīhi minal-haqqi bi-idhnik, innaka tahdī man tashāu' ilā sirātim-mustaqīm

O Allah, Lord of Jibraīl, Mikaīl and Israfil. Creator of the heavens and the earth, Knower of the Unseen and Seen. You judge between Your slaves in what they differ with each other. Guide me with Your permission to where I diverge from the truth, as You guide those You wish to the straight path.

Source: Muslim

---

(85)

رَبَّنَـا لَا تُـزِغْ قُلُوبَنَـا بَعْدَ إِذْ هَدَيْتَنَا وَهَـبْ لَنَا مِنْ لَدُنْكَ رَحْمَةً إِنَّكَ أَنْتَ الوَهَّابُ

Rabbanā la tuzigh qulūbanā b'ada idh hadaytanā wa hab lanā min ladunka rahmatan innaka antal-wahhab

Our Lord, let not our hearts deviate after You have guided us
and grant us from Yourself mercy.
Indeed, You are the Bestower.

Source: Quran (3:8)

---

(86)

اللهـم انفَعْنِي بِما عَلَّمْتَنِـي وعَلِّمْنِي ما يَنْفَعُنِي وزِدْنِي عِلْمًا
الْحَمْدُ لِلَّهِ عَلَى كُلِّ حَالٍ وَأَعُوذُ بِاللَّهِ مِنْ حَالِ أَهْلِ النَّارِ

*Allāhummanfa'nī bimā 'allamtanī wa 'allimnī mā yanfa'unī
wa zidnī 'ilman alhamdulilāhi 'alā kulli hāl,
wa a'ūdhu billāhi min hālin-nār*

O Allah, benefit me from what You have taught me and teach
me that which will benefit me and increase me in knowledge.
All praise is due to Allah in every condition, and I seek refuge
in Allah from the condition of the people of the Fire.

Source: al-Tirmidhi

---

(87)

اللَّهمَّ اهدِني فيمَن هدَيتَ، وعافِني فيمَن عافَيتَ، وتَوَلَّنِي فيمَن تولَّيتَ، وبارِكْ لي
فيـما أعطَيتَ، وقِني شرَّ ما قضَيتَ، فإنَّكَ تَقضي ولا يُقضى عليك، وإنه لا يَذِلُّ مَن
والَيتَ، تبارَكتَ ربَّنا وتعالَيتَ

*Allāhummahdinī fiman hadayt, wa 'āfinī fiman 'āfayt, wa
tawallanī fiman tawallayt, wa bārik lī fīmā 'atayt, wa qinī
sharra mā qadayt, innaka taqdī wa lā yuqdā 'alayk, wa innahu
lā yadhillu man wā layt, wa lā ya'izzu man 'ādayt, tabārakta
rabbanā wa ta'ālayt*

O Allah, guide me amongst those You have guided, and grant
me security amongst those to whom You granted security,
and grant me guardianship amongst those to whom You have
granted guardianship, and bless me in whatever You have
bestowed upon me, and protect me from any evil that You
have ordained. Indeed, You decree (for others) and nothing

is decreed for You. None that You take care of is humiliated, and none that You take as enemy is honoured. Blessed and Exalted are You, O Lord.

Source: Abu-Dawud

---

(88)

رَبَّنَا آتِنَا فِي الدُّنْيَا حَسَنَةً وَفِي الْآخِرَةِ حَسَنَةً وَقِنَا عَذَابَ النَّارِ

Rabbanā ātinā fid-dunyā hasanatan wa fil-ākhirati hasanatan wa qinā 'athāban-nār

Our Lord, give us in this world that which is good and in the Hereafter that which is good, and save us from the punishment of the Fire.

Source: Quran (2:201)

---

(89)

رَبِّ هَبْ لِي حُكْمًا وَأَلْحِقْنِي بِالصَّالِحِينَ
وَاجْعَلْ لِي لِسَانَ صِدْقٍ فِي الْآخِرِينَ
وَاجْعَلْنِي مِنْ وَرَثَةِ جَنَّةِ النَّعِيمِ

Rabbi hab lī hukman wal-hiqnī bis-salihīn
Waj'al lī lisāna sidqin fil-ākhirīn
Waj'alnī min wa rathati jannatin-na'īm

My Lord, grant me authority and join me with the righteous. And grant me a reputation of honour among later generations. And place me among the inheritors of the Garden of Pleasure.

Source: Quran (26:83-85)

---

(90)

اللَّهُمَّ اجْعَلْ فِي قَلْبِي نُورًا، وَفِي بَصَرِي نُورًا، وَفِي سَمْعِي نُورًا، وَعَنْ يَمِينِي نُورًا، وَعَنْ يَسَارِي نُورًا، وَفَوْقِي نُورًا، وَتَحْتِي نُورًا، وَأَمَامِي نُورًا، وَخَلْفِي نُورًا، وَاجْعَلْ لِي نُورًا

Allāhummaj'al fī qalbī nūrā, wa fī basarī nūrā, wa fī sam'ī nūrā, wa 'an yamīnī nūrā, wa 'an yasārī nūrā, wa-fawqī nūrā wa tahtī nūrā, wa amāmī nūrā, wa khalfī nūrā, waj'al lī nūrā

O Allah, place light in my heart and light in my sight and light in my hearing and light on my right side and light on my left side and light above me and light below me and light ahead of me and light behind me, and make me from light.

Source: al-Bukhari

---

(91)

رَبِّ إِنِّي لِمَا أَنزَلْتَ إِلَيَّ مِنْ خَيْرٍ فَقِيرٌ

Rabbi innī limā anzalta ilayya min khayrin faqīr

My Lord, indeed I am, for whatever good You would send down to me, in need.

Source: Quran (28:24)

---

(92)

اللَّهُمَّ أَلْهِمْنِي رُشْدِي وَأَعِذْنِي مِنْ شَرِّ نَفْسِي

Allāhummal-himnī rushdī wa a'idhnī min sharri nafsī

O Allāh, inspire me to be rightly guided and protect me from the evil of myself.

Source: al-Tirmidhi and Ahmad

---

(93)

رَبِّ أَوْزِعْنِي أَنْ أَشْكُرَ نِعْمَتَكَ الَّتِي أَنْعَمْتَ عَلَيَّ وَعَلَى وَالِدَيَّ وَأَنْ أَعْمَلَ صَالِحًا تَرْضَاهُ وَأَصْلِحْ لِي فِي ذُرِّيَّتِي إِنِّي تُبْتُ إِلَيْكَ وَإِنِّي مِنَ الْمُسْلِمِينَ

Rabbi awz'inī an ashkura n'imatakal-latī an'amta 'alayya wa 'alā wālidayya wa an 'amala sālihan tardāhu wa aslih lī fī dhurriyyatī innī tubtu ilayka wa innī minal-muslimīn

My Lord, enable me to be grateful for Your favor which You have bestowed upon me and upon my parents and to work righteousness of which You will approve and make righteous for me my offspring. Indeed, I have repented to You, and indeed, I am of the Muslims.

Source: Quran (46:15)

---

(94)

رَبَّنَا أَتْمِمْ لَنَا نُورَنَا وَاغْفِرْ لَنَا إِنَّكَ عَلَىٰ كُلِّ شَيْءٍ قَدِيرٌ

*Rabbanā atmim lanā nūranā waghfir lanā
innaka 'ala kulli shayi'n qadīr*

Our Lord, perfect for us our light and forgive us. Indeed, You are over all things competent.

Source: Quran (66:8)

---

(95)

رَبِّ زِدْنِي عِلْمًا

Rabbi zidnī 'ilmā

My Lord, increase me in knowledge.

Source: Quran (20:114)

---

(96)

رَبِّ هَبْ لِي مِن لَّدُنكَ ذُرِّيَّةً طَيِّبَةً إِنَّكَ سَمِيعُ الدُّعَاءِ

Rabbi hab lī min ladunka thurriyyatan tayyibatan innaka samī'ud-du'ā

My Lord, grant me from Yourself a good offspring. Indeed, You are the Hearer of supplication.

Source: Quran (3:38)

---

(97)

رَبِّ لَا تَذَرْنِي فَرْدًا وَأَنتَ خَيْرُ الْوَارِثِينَ

Rabbi lā tadharnī fardan wa anta khayrul-wārithīn

My Lord, do not leave me alone [with no heir], while you are the best of inheritors.

Source: Quran (21:89)

---

(98)

رَبِّ هَبْ لِي مِنَ الصَّالِحِينَ

Rabbi hab lī minas-sālihīn

My Lord, grant me [a child] from among the righteous.

Source: Quran (37:100)

---

(99)

رَبَّنَا هَبْ لَنَا مِنْ أَزْوَاجِنَا وَذُرِّيَّاتِنَا قُرَّةَ أَعْيُنٍ وَاجْعَلْنَا لِلْمُتَّقِينَ إِمَامًا

Rabbanā hab lanā min azwājinā wa dhurriyyātinā qurrata 'ayunin waj'alnā lilmuttaqīna imāmā

Our Lord, grant us from among our wives and offspring comfort to our eyes and make us an example for the righteous.

Source: Quran (25:74)

---

(100)

ربنا تقبل منا إنك أنت السميع العليم

Rabbanā taqabbal minnā innaka antas-samī'ul-'alīm

Our Lord, accept [this] from us. Indeed, You are the Hearing, the Knowing.

Source: Quran (2:127)

ALSO AVAILABLE BY LIGHT PUBLISHING

www.ingramcontent.com/pod-product-compliance
Lightning Source LLC
Chambersburg PA
CBHW011959090526
44590CB00023B/3788